Abdullayeva Ra'no Tajiboyevna

Commonwealth of Nations

© Taemeer Publications LLC
Commonwealth of Nations
by: Abdullayeva Ra'no Tajiboyevna

Edition: February '2024
Publisher:
Taemeer Publications LLC (Michigan, USA / Hyderabad, India)

© Taemeer Publications

Book : Commonwealth of Nations
Author : Abdullayeva Ra'no Tajiboyevna
Publisher : Taemeer Publications
Year : '2024
Pages : 42
Title Design : *Taemeer Web Design*

Hakimova Muborak was born on June 18, 1979 in Uchkurgan district of Namangan region. Head of the Department of Library Information Activities at the Institute of Arts and Culture of Uzbekistan.

The place and role of fiction in the formation of reading culture in elementary school students

Annotation: To attract elementary school students to read a scientific article, it is necessary to select modern literature written taking into account their age characteristics. Are revised every two to three years, in addition, it is necessary to take into account the unique characteristics of each region, its creators and their creativity, that any work of art written for children must be adapted to their age and level, it must be suitable, moreover, in their deep thoughts must be awakened in hearts and minds and called to noble ends.

Key words: Socialization, literary traditions, new spiritual space, artistic culture, public discussion, critical thinking, worldview, tolerance, cultural heritage, media environment, reading culture.

For several centuries, the books read in childhood played the main role in the socialization of a person, but today this situation has undergone great changes. The status of a person who reads has decreased, and now visual culture, not books, is playing the main role in the process of children's socialization. But in educated families, the high role of the book remains. Of course, this refers to the role and importance of fiction books in the formation of a person. However, new studies show that today the role of fiction as a socializing tool is declining. This applies primarily to classical literature. Propagation and transmission of works of classics and 20th-century artists to generations belongs more to families with private libraries. But recently, the number of such families is decreasing. It is necessary to adopt new educational programs for families, schools and libraries so that such literary traditions do not stop completely. Also, taking into account the fact that the current generation is growing up in a new spiritual space and environment, it is necessary to study their interests and needs.

It is known that the acceptance of artistic culture in many cases is not directly through the advice of adults, but through books and reading environment.

Recent research suggests that even in the Internet age, the personal library environment has a major impact on elementary school students' reading ability. In addition, the personal library environment has a positive effect not only on traditional reading, but also on the use of the Internet. In order to attract elementary school students to reading, it is necessary to select modern literature written taking into account their age characteristics. For this purpose, it is necessary to attract specialists-experts-philologists, literary critics, librarian-bibliographers, school library staff who understand modern literature. Before handing over to the experts, it is necessary to hold a public discussion and this situation should be reviewed every two to three years. In addition, it is necessary to take into account the characteristics of each region, its creators, and their creativity.

Since there are so many children's books (including translations) being published today, it is necessary to select them carefully.

Specialists should pay attention to the following when acquiring books for the library fund:

- Separation of publications according to specific purpose and intended users;

- The team of authors (scientists, popularizers, unspecified personnel);

- Decorated with age-appropriate illustrations of users;

- Artistic value (various reviews in the press, mention in various sources).

In most children's libraries and school libraries, the main evaluation criteria are:

- Reputation, popularity, trust index of author, publisher;

- Reviews and evaluations of specialists, experts;

- Readability of books;

- Compliance with spiritual and moral standards, artistic aesthetic characteristics;

- Newness of the topic and relevance of the issues raised in the book;

- User survey;

- Parents' ratings.

In particular, when compiling a list of recommendations on the topic "We advise elementary school students to read", the main attention should be paid to the following:

1. It is created with high artistic skills.

2. An accurate representation of reality, regardless of whether it is implemented in a realistic or fantastic form.

3. Setting difficult problems.

4. Forming a positive attitude towards life.

5. Being able to attract according to the plot.

6. Positive evaluation by professional teams, press, users.

7. Having received foreign or local awards.

In modern literature, children's literature is described as follows:

• children of senior preschool age (4-6 years old);

• children of junior school age (7-10 years old);

• children of secondary school age (11-15 years old);

• children of senior school age (16-17 years old) [5. B.144].

Children's literature is characterized by the following features:

• giving the main role to children;

• appropriateness of children's age on the topic;

• relatively small size, decorated with pictures;

• simplicity of language;

• less images, more communication and behavior;

• wealth of adventures;

• positive ending (victory of goodness over evil);

• the main goal is to educate a person [8 B. 126].

Children's books published in developed countries are subject to the following criteria:

- bright and interesting presentation in literate language, enriching the lexicon of its readers;

- develop thinking, including critical thinking, expand worldview;

- enrichment of human emotions, moral development, teaching children empathy. Calls for tolerance and goodness;

- prepare for life, create a model of behavior in complex conditions;

- to expand the possibility of self-knowledge;

- create the ability to understand other cultures and people;

- understanding of other generations, formation of solidarity with them;

- creates a relationship to cultural heritage;

- to have value as a work of art;

- to have value as a value to people belonging to other cultures.

Any artistic work written for children must be appropriate for their age and level. Moreover, it should awaken deep thoughts in their hearts and minds, and call them to noble goals. The famous English writer Joanna Rowling's children's book series about Harry Potter and his friends took a large place in the lives of young people in the 2000s. To do, to find strength in difficult situations, not to sell friends, not to discuss others, to understand that freedom is a wonderful attraction, to understand that life without love is not life, to understand that fighting for goodness is necessary at any age. Although there are generally enough children's books being published, not all of them are of good quality. Therefore, one of the difficult tasks facing the school library staff is the formation of the ability to analyze the quality of children's books based on the possibilities of their reception by young users. Studying the sociodynamics of the reading process in our country shows that reading is undergoing a certain transformation recently. Even though elementary school students are reading books less, they are using the internet more often. Because now the Internet is changing not only the speed of reading, but also the motivation of reading. At the same time, the development of visual culture, the ability to use the Internet and social networks is shaping the limitation of surface reading to reading excerpts from the main text. The reading repertoire is also changing, reading "easy to digest" books for more relaxation. In the 20th century, the works and literary traditions that formed the basis of family reading of several generations and were loved by children are becoming a thing of the past. A factor influencing children's reading is social networks and various sources of information on the Internet. As we mentioned above, as a result of the ongoing transformation process, the use of electronic text instead of paper text is becoming more evident. In addition to changes in the media environment, the existence of a "book environment" related to the ability of libraries to provide their users with new and interesting books affects not only print products, but also children's reading on the Internet and social networks. Even in today's information overload environment, a developed book environment and school libraries have the potential to influence the reading of elementary school students. Today, school libraries are not only the preservers of cultural traditions related to reading, but also provide children with the best quality books.

It is known that it is possible to raise a literate reader only in childhood, but children with high reading literacy and culture are formed in an environment where there are selected books and literate adults. Today, the reading habits of the growing generation are changing intensively and this process continues. The results of the conducted research show that today school libraries remain a social institution that effectively adapts to the changing information space. As we mentioned above, the fact that the role of fiction in the socialization of a person is decreasing is related to many factors, first of all, it depends on the changing market media environment. Children's reading is significantly influenced by the products of the visual culture market. Computer games, cartoons, TV series, children's movies reduce the time they need to read. Today, creating books for elementary school students has also become a global problem. Along with the best children's books, artistically weak literature is also being published. In addition, the very few copies of the best children's books prevent them from reaching everyone. Quality assessment of children's books also remains a problem.

In our opinion, it is necessary for the staff of school libraries to get acquainted not only with the books recognized as the best, but also with the books that are included in the list of low-quality books, but also with the books that are read with interest by elementary school students for some reason [6. B.18].

Today, the role of school library staff as experts who can find information and books that can be recommended for elementary school students, and who can critically evaluate them is increasing. In particular, it is related to the best and necessary literature recommended for children and their parents.

Currently, the demands placed on the quality of education expect changes from the staff of school libraries.

In conclusion, I can say that, firstly, in the conditions of declining role of classical literature in student education, pedagogues and librarians should look for new ways to strengthen reading motivation; Second, the joining forces of education and librarianship professionals should be motivated by the need to encourage reading among elementary school students; Thirdly, the main goal should be to attract them to read the best books published in our country and abroad.

Studying the experience of our country and abroad shows that if the school libraries are well equipped and able to provide the necessary services for students, they will have a special reputation among the community and parents. Even in today's Internet age, the fact that libraries are being used shows that they have a place in the process of continuous education.

Used literature:

1. Mirziyoev Sh.M. Development strategy of new Uzbekistan. Third edition.- Tashkent: Publishing House of Uzbekistan, 2022.- 440 pages.

2. Decree of the President of the Republic of Uzbekistan on the establishment of a commission on the development of the system of printing and distribution of book products, on the promotion and promotion of book reading and reading culture. January 12, 2017.

3. Decision of the President of the Republic of Uzbekistan on the program of measures of the commission on the development of the system of publishing and distribution of book products, increasing and promoting the culture of book reading and reading. September 13, 2017.

4. Decision of the President of the Republic of Uzbekistan on the further formation of information-library services to the

population of the Republic of Uzbekistan. June 7, 2019.

5. Ghaziev E. Methodology of psychology. Tashkent: Teacher, 2007.-346 p.

6. Yoldoshev E. Guiding children's reading in the library.-Tashkent: Uzbekistan, 2002.-128 p.

7. Melenteva Yu.P. Obshchaya theory chteniya. Moscow, Nauka, 2015.-230 p.

8. Melenteva Yu.P. Chtenie: yavlenie, process, deyatelnost. Moscow, Nauka, 2018.-282 p.

1. 9. Chudinova V.P. Razvitie natsiy chitateley v raznyx stranax mira: issledovaniya, strategii, proekty, praktiki. Moscow, Kniga, 2014.-344 p.
2. 10. Umarov A.O. Reading culture: Person, society, development.-Tashkent: Fan, 2004.-194 p.
3. 11. Philosophy: An encyclopedic dictionary.-Tashkent: "Sharq" NMAK Chief Editorial Office, 2004.-469 p.

Khurshid Ne'mat was born on May 28, 1986 in Kesakli neighborhood of Olot district of Bukhara region. 2nd year (external) student of Bukhara State University, Faculty of Journalism. So far, 4 books have been published ("Qadr", "The Bitter Pain of Missing", "Colors of the Heart", "Maple in Kesakli"). His poems and articles have been published in regional and national newspapers and magazines. Currently, he is working as a youth leader in the Olot district branch of the Youth Affairs Agency.

TASHKENT

The roads are congested, two or three at night.

The lights don't go out until dawn.

Different nationalities keep coming.

How noisy Tashkent is.

Its buildings are like stars at night.

If you want to be a witness, come and go!

Night is like day.

Tashkent does not sleep for a moment.

Azim city, old bread city.

You will find peace, a city.

A generous, honorable city.

Tashkent teaches climbing.

Honestly, I don't want to leave you.

Come on, it's really different.

Accept your food and salt from me.

Stay safe, Tashkent!

MY HOUSE

Mother, watch your son's house,

Let's go to your house.

I restored the foundations of poems,

I set a rhyme to the new song.

Door-frames made of meaning,

Rain, snow and humidity that do not lose color.

Every roof covered with words,

Don't worry, even in an earthquake.

Bright lights – a fairy of inspiration,

A lamp that lights up the whole building.

Everything shines in the night and does not go out,

The wall is elegantly painted in pencil.

The thick gate is made of heavy weight,

I knitted the fence from the string.

I didn't get money from any poet,

I know the torture of debt.

I did not build a stone, making a double floor,

Maybe it's luck that laughed at me.

I drew a draft,

This is the house of Khurshid Nemat.

AUTHOR: MALIKA USMONOVA

***

Don't let life crush me

My mother is salty.

He doesn't say a word, but

They feel it from their eyes.

If I get a nick on my heel,

Sinks into his heart.

In Khadikli's eyes,

White dawns...

Make the four of me happy,

Do not despair.

My child...

My child...

As my child

Don't get sick.

God bless me.

Make my life long.

Be happy with me

And long live...!

FATHER

You played father yesterday in your sail,

I am in your prayers today.

The years threw me away

I am in the royal palace.

My words that I could never say,

I put it on my black eyes.

I miss him in my heart,

I poured it into your heart.

Am I enough, Ota, to appreciate you?

I can't be a support if you stumble.

I silently warm to your eyes,

I don't know how you feel!

Curses hung on your black hair,

You don't seem to care.

What trials have come to your dear head,

You can't see anyone else, my friend.

Father, if you don't tell me you hurt me,

When I ask how you are, you say leave me alone.

You still bear the burden of bread,

When do you think of yourself?

Father, don't let me go

My name does not come from your lips.

May your prayers protect me

Not a single moment of me will pass without you!

Abdullayeva Rano Tajiboy's daughter was born on May 14, 1991 in the Amudarya district of the Republic of Karakalpakstan. Her poems were published in "Sharq Yulduzi" magazine from "Yangi Sirdaryo", "Ustoz" newspapers, in the anthology "Turan Edibleri" published in Turkey and in the anthology "Turan Edibleri 2" published in Kyrgyzstan. Collector and compiler of the anthology "Eastern rains". Member of the creative association "World Talents" in Kazakhstan. Currently, she is a student of the State Institute of Art and Culture of Uzbekistan.

LIBRARY SCIENCE

When we start talking about the library, we are not talking about yesterday, but about thousands of years of history. Because this profession is very ancient and, in addition to its antiquity, it can be said to be a very delicate profession.

From our attitude to our facial expressions, our greeting directly affects visitors. Especially for children and teenagers. Children get bored quickly, but teenagers are very impressionable during the transition period. In this case, a polite, sincere smile and, of course, patience are required from the librarian. We always think of a librarian as ordinary. Because our school librarian teachers are stuck in our imagination. But now this style cannot be accepted by the youth of today. Now we need to come up with a modern look. The reason is that today's children are very smart and demanding. They require a lot of information from us. It is very difficult to impress them. The rapid exchange of information is speeding up time and making children grow up prematurely. For this reason, if you observe children, you can observe that they quickly get bored with their surroundings and events. That's why they love speed. In such a situation, it is a very difficult task to get them interested in books and bring them to the library. To change the situation, first of all, it is necessary to work with their parents. Because the atmosphere at home has a strong influence on the child's psyche. Whenever a child sees a book at home or sees a parent flipping through a book, it instills a love for books in the child's brain. Because for every child, parents are their ideal. It's a good activity if they read a book. A visit to the library under the guidance of parents is another good option. A bird does what it sees in its nest. What did we say? This is one of the methods of library science. Now we are in an age where we forget the old views that "this tactic is not right for us". It's past time for us to put our skills in numbers. It's time to prove how strong a specialist we are with a crowd of readers. First of all, we need to remove the wall that I am an expert, these are ordinary readers and readers, and talk to readers as readers. We must increase our vigilance and be careful. We should be interested in why he chose this particular book, whether it was his choice or someone's recommendation. We may not be interested in the truth, but conversations like this will boost their confidence in their choices. If we ourselves recommend some literature, the awkwardness between the student and the librarian will be removed. We will achieve our goal only if this conversation is not official, but very sincere and friendly. Every reader is a closed world and we need to be able to enter that world. This is why library science requires psychology from us. In addition to books, the library must have flowers, even a few balloons and toys of any kind. Because children do not understand formality. They need comfort, and these items can directly convey an emotion to adults that you might not have thought possible. The concept of children's reading has two different meanings. The concept of children's reading has two different meanings. In a broad sense, the phenomenon of children's reading is the reading of all literary, artistic, scientific and popular works intended for them to read. However, in the period when there were no examples of creations dedicated to children, the reading among adults, which has been going on for a long time, tried to read short stories or didactic works, which can be noted as the first appearance of children's reading. Safo Matchonov commented on children's reading: "...reading in a narrow sense means reading books, but in a broad sense it includes the concepts of selective reading, feeling, understanding and expressing opinions. "It is nourished by fiction and expands with the support of literary criticism and pedagogy," he writes. In fact, literacy refers to reading books in both broad and narrow sense. Therefore, even though "Book" sounds differently in different languages, it essentially expresses the same concept. There is also a librarian. When leaving the library, putting the electronic version of the book he has read on his phone, assigning him to continue the book from where he left it, and giving him a small gift or even a simple sweet, if he finishes reading, encouraging the child will give a world of motivation.

Muhammad Diyor Shavkatjonov was born on November 5, 2002 in Kuva district of Fergana region.

Association of artists "Dormon", A member of the International Union of Poets-Writers "Double Wing" of the Republic of Kazakhstan. The first samples of creativity were published in "Kuva life", "Ulug' El", "Teaching in Uzbekistan", "Bekajon" and a number of different newspapers and magazines of our republic. His poems were published in "Hilal II", "Hilal III", "Yurak mavjlari" poetry collections, and in the Turkish anthology "Sozlerim". He is the absolute winner of the "Student of the Year-2023" competition in the nomination "The most active creative student of the year". He creates poetry in the genres of verse, uchshoda, couplet, and ghazal. His poems have been translated into English, Turkish, and Kyrgyz languages. "Uchshodalar Bayozi", composed of writers from Central Asian countries, is about to be published in the Kyrgyz-Uzbek anthology, which includes writers from Turkic countries.

The holder of "Ahmed Yassavi", "For International Services", "Pride of the Nation" badges, and the title of "Served Artist" founded by the International Association of Poets-Writers of the Republic of Kazakhstan "Qosh qanot".

Winner of more than 30 international and republican contests held among young people.

Currently, he is a 4th-year student of the Faculty of Mechanical Engineering of Fergana Polytechnic Institute.

EVERY NIGHT HAS A MORNING

(Story)

Tired from the field, Shahodat entered the house and lowered her from his shoulder. She wiped the sweat from his forehead with a handkerchief and sighed. At the edge of the yard, her little girl was playing in the sand. Her sons Sadiq and Salih drove the flock to the mountain.

"They must still come," he thought. She immediately started to eat dinner. The husband will still come. Hoynahoy went back to

Baqi Mullah's house on the outskirts of the neighborhood. These people are also interesting! From morning till night they gather in this mullah's house and discuss something. One of them was beaten by her husband, and the other's wife cheated on her husband. Another had a child or a loved one with a terminal illness. He has so many pains. Shouldn't we gather ourselves together and face the Creator in prayer?

With such different thoughts, Shahadat put fire in the furnace. It's not easy for him either. She has to support her three children and her husband as well. The money he earned by plowing the fields and working as a wage laborer was not enough. If she finds it in the stomach of her children, he doesn't have it on him, if he finds it on him, he won't go to school.

In fact, I could have done what my mother told me and divorced this wretched husband 10 years ago, - said Shahodat and began to think again. But it was good that they didn't divorce. If they had divorced, she wouldn't have a sweet little girl now. Because she had children, she put up with her husband's various insults and brutal beatings. By the way, if there were no babies, would he have already collected all his food?!

The sun, rising in a fiery hue from a distance, is sinking more and more behind the rocks. The sound of mother's cows is also heard, while her sons are bringing the herd. Before the cows entered the barn, Shahodat pulled the coals from the stove and walked towards the barn carrying the bucket. At that moment, the gate opened, and her husband Arif entered on an old, discolored bicycle, with disheveled hair and dusty clothes. Shahadat immediately put down the bucket and went to set the table. If she didn't put food in front of her husband now, it was certain that her husband would scold her. He prepared food for them and went to the farm again with a bucket.

After milking the cows, he put the bucket on a tree branch and sat down to eat. After eating, she turned to her husband, who was lying on his side watching TV, and began to speak in fear:

"Daddy, now you could reduce your walks a little and help with the household." If the days get colder, the work in the fields stops, and I don't go to work, how will we survive? Our daughter Saodat will also go to school this year. She also became a big girl. Your sons are no longer young. "We can't give them better clothes," said her husband, contradicting her.

God provides for children. As soon as we ran away, my Lord will not give us a difficult wife,' he said, getting up to go into the room. Besides, Mullah Baqi said that soon we will get rich, we will buy one of the luxury houses at the beginning of the neighborhood, one great car, and we will live happily. According to Shahadat husband:

- The creator also gives to the servant who acts. We can't sit like this and say, "Eat an apple, put it in my mouth." There is a saying that "action from you is blessing from me"...

"He will give it, he will give it one day anyway," said Arif. Sharafat became uncomfortable:

"After all," her husband shouted angrily:

- That's enough, don't teach me. Am I the head of this house or you? He slammed the door and entered the house. Sharofat sighed and stayed in the cattle for a while, thinking.

After that, the mornings began to rise and the days began to set. Although years have passed, Arif's habit has not changed. He still spends his days at that mullah's house. This year, his son Salih will graduate from school and enter university. At home, there are daily beatings and quarrels. Shahadat's eyes are still bruised, his lips are still pale. Shahadat, who has been enduring the husband's beatings for so many years, could not endure it this year. Arif did not want to teach Saleh. "It costs a lot of money to teach for 4 years." Today, this topic was opened again, and a quarrel broke out at home again. Shahadat stubbornly insisted that he would educate his son. In fact, it is better if their sons are educated and have enough bread, so that tomorrow they will not be dependent on someone else.

"Are you still going to take my word for it?" said Arif, shaking Shahodat. There was no place left unbeaten. This was their last fight. Because Shahadat no longer wants to live with this man.

Seeing the children being beaten by their parents, their love for their father decreases. They did not want to live with their father. Sometimes they cried with tears in their eyes because they were afraid of their father's quarrels. Seeing this, the eldest son Saleh decided to make his mother the happiest woman in the world. Over time, their lives improved. His son Salih entered school. They bought a small, cozy house in the city. It is as if the difficulties of martyrdom are behind. Now he does not plow the fields, he does not work as a hired laborer. The person who brings the family into the light is only the child. Salih and Sadiq is a smart boy. They do not leave their mother alone. In time, if they get married, their family will expand even more. They marry his sister. Their desire to live with such a dream and actions corresponding to that dream increased and they began to live life. It is said that "Every night has a morning." The darkest part of the night is an hour before dawn. If our life has become dark, it means that the dawn will come soon. There is no doubt about it.

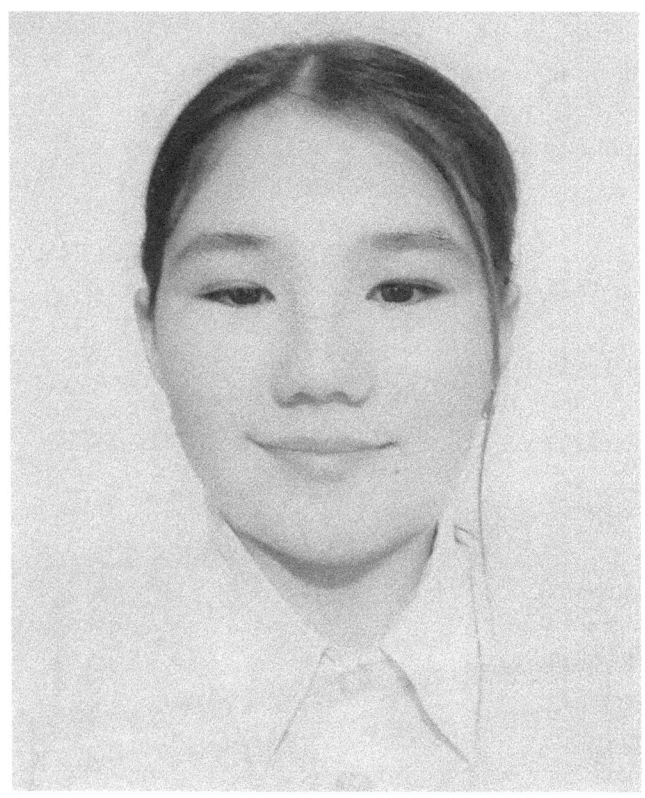

Abdukakhhorova Dilnura is a 9th grade student of the 54th general secondary school of Andijan district. She studies at the Andijan School of Young Journalists. In her free time, she is engaged in creativity. In the future, receiving a state award named after Zulfia. She took an active part in several anthologies and participated in the anthologies organized in Uzbekistan with his works. Shine Girls Academy season 1 contestant. "Future Science Girls Education Exchange Program" is a season 12 graduate.

***

Your bright future my country,

Our independent country.

Restless youth,

Tomorrow's successor.

The youth of Uzbekistan

We are advanced in every field.

Education or art,

Never be jealous.

The youth of Uzbekistan

We have a great future.

We will always build together,

The prospect of tomorrow.

We will be young people!

MY BROTHER

Caressed from my youth,

Carefully.

Someone is upset,

You are the one who gave the punishment.

I'm still a man,

I do not know the value.

I smile when I remember,

The flower you gave me.

Don't stop saying brother, brother,

I followed you.

Even so, he said,

You looked into my heart.

My dear brother,

Be happy.

If it's not you, I don't even,

It's like I don't exist in this world.

Mingboyeva Zulhayo was born on March 28, 2008 in Khavos district of Syrdarya region. Currently, she is a 9th-grade student of creative school named after Halima Khudoyberdiyeva. The first book was published under the name

"Koklam Song". Her poems are included in "Bouquet from the Garden of Creativity", "Songs of the Heart", "Songs of the Golden Generation" and in the anthology "Mujde" published by "Baygench" publishing house of the Republic of Turkey. Her scientific articles have been published in magazines of several countries such as USA, France, Russia, Germany, Denmark. Her creative works are constantly published in a number of newspapers, such as "Yangi Sirdaryo", "Morning Star", "Marifat", "Literature and Art of Uzbekistan", "Fergana Haqiqiti", "Sugd Haqiqiti" of the Republic of Tajikistan.

***

White evening...

The meeting time of eyelashes,

Eyes turn blue,

Say the word...

Quadrupeds – unchained howl,

The earth tickles his bosom.

The ground groans,

My shoulder is in pain.

The pain is exposed,

When I shout

Sounds...

He wrote on the paper saying happiness.

If I crumpled and stomped on my feet,

To compensate for the

Smallpox covered.

When I comb my hair,

Huuv willow root is a thick sucker.

I'm not afraid. Now your heart

A hearty meal...

I have a feeling in my soul,

It's been a while since I returned to the wilderness.

Eyes turn blue,

Say the word...

THE WORD WILL

(Dedication to Erkin Vohidov)

The ground is rotten,

Good morning.

They said that you will be born in the world.

I didn't want to say anything.

One step from me to you

One point is our witness.

Poetry in the palm of his hand,

It is will that grows, it is oh.

The invisible end of the point,

All my strength is captive to silence.

Cheeks become puffy,

Afraid to look in the mirror.

My pains are getting old,

It's not the road that blows your mind.

I lived staring at the paper,

Your hands wrote in my eyes man!

Your hands wrote in my eyes man!

Nazirova Nargiza was born on May 15, 2009 in Peshku District, Bukhara Region. Currently, she is studying in the 9th "A" class of the Specialized School of the Presidential Educational Agency in Peshku District. With the help of Vahidov Bakhtiyor, her first book called "Vatan manzumasi" and two poems were published in "Smile" magazine, in the book "Development of Uzbek Turk edediyatının – 2" in Turkish and in several other newspapers.

SPRING SORROW

Spring. You came again, knocking on my door,

You brought a dream with you.

I like you very much

I regretted when you left.

My heart is full of pain,

A little more than apricot blossoms.

Bearman years that hurt me

Please let me know if there are any objections.

Spring. You came to my garden again

Your gentle wind caresses my hair.

And the white cloud in the sky

Everyone knows my pains.

My spring, I missed you a lot.

I am very happy to see you today.

My sick broken heart

I forgot the pain.

I used to say that I love flowers,

He is crying with his head bowed.

Someone who won't leave me

Loneliness always haunts me.

Come spring leaves of youth,

Don't stop flying over my head.

Now back to me the past years,

Don't talk about past dreams.

Spring. Time is passing again.

You will leave again without a trace, without a picture.

Autumn, Winter, Summer even,

You don't want to be with me.

I'll wait another year,

My heart is full of pain until you come.

In fact, this is the pen that writes poetry

My pains will end without writing.

Spring. Come again, knock on my door,

I can't find you, I'm a wanderer.

I like you very much

My heart is broken when you leave.

ONCE GIVEN A CHANCE TO DIE...

Once given the chance to die,

I took to the field as a brave man.

This world is a land of sadness and sorrow,

My eyes are full of tears, my heart is full.

That's not why I'm dying

I just want to know who is friend and who is enemy.

Is this a difficult choice to make?

No, I don't wish for a heart with my thoughts.

Let's say I'm dead, the coffin is dark

Everyone is crying with tears in their eyes.

Dark sadness covered the sky,

Look, who are they laughing?

Was there an earthquake? No, my mother.

He is kicking the ground and crying.

That empty room of mine, which is humming today,

My poems scratch his heart.

All are suffering, but never,

It is impossible to persuade my father.

Did I need that old soul

Can I think of my father?

My eyes are dark, my heart is restless,

I cried every night because someone needed me.

I always miss my parents.

Crying and begging God, this is the day.

That's it, that's it, I forgot, don't remind me

I will never die, I will always live.

Can someone tell me again?

I'm waiting for that revenge.

www.ingramcontent.com/pod-product-compliance
Lightning Source LLC
LaVergne TN
LVHW010416070526
838199LV00064B/5321